In All
the Rooms
of the
Yellow
House

In All
the Rooms
of the
Yellow
House

Nancy Mairs

A Blue Moon and Confluence Press Book

WINNER OF THE 1984 WESTERN STATES BOOK AWARD IN POETRY

Sponsored by the Western States Arts Foundation in Santa Fe, New Mexico, The Western States Book Awards are presented to outstanding authors and publishers of fiction, short fiction, creative non-fiction, and poetry. Jurors for 1984 were: Robert Penn Warren, Jonathan Galassi, Carolyn Kizer, Al Young, and Jack Shoemaker. The Western States Arts Foundation Book Awards are organized by the Western States Arts Foundation with funding from The Xerox Foundation, the B. Dalton Bookseller, and the National Endowment for the Arts.

Some of the poems in this volume originally appeared in The Academy of American Poets *Selections 1973–78*; *Anima* (ANIMA Publications, 1053 Wilson Avenue, Chambersburg, PA 17201), *Greenhouse Review, The Louisville Review, Mazagine,* and *Prickly Pear*. Others appeared in the Maguey Press chapbook entitled *Instead It Is Winter*, Rolly Kent, series editor.

Publication of *In All The Rooms of the Yellow House* is made possible, in part, by the Arizona Commission on the Arts and Humanities, Western States Arts Foundation, and Confluence Press at Lewis-Clark State College in Lewiston, Idaho. The publisher also acknowledges the generous and long-standing individual patronage of Clint Colby.

ISBN: Cloth 0-933188-26-9.   Paper 0-933188-27-7

Distributed to the trade by: Kampmann & Company, Inc., 9 East 40 Street, New York 10016.

About the Author...Nancy Mairs was born, by accident of war, in Long Beach, California, in 1943. She grew up in Exeter, New Hampshire, and Wenham, Massachusetts, spending part of each summer in her great-grandmother's yellow house in Kennebunkport, Maine. She received the A.B. *cum laude* in English literature from Wheaton College in 1964. From 1966 to 1972 she worked as a technical editor at the Smithsonian Astrophysical Observatory, the MIT Press, and the International Tax Program of the Harvard Law School. She then moved to Arizona and spent the next eleven years teaching high-school and college composition courses and doing graduate work, taking the M.F.A. in creative writing (poetry) from The University of Arizona in 1975. Currently, she is completing the Ph.D. in English. She has a collection of personal essays written from a feminist perspective forthcoming from the University of Arizona Press. Currently, she works as a project director in the Southwest Institute for Research on Women in Tucson where she lives with her husband and children.

for Jean Pedrick

"Gradually she came to see that life on earth was unavoidable."

C. J. Jung, *Memories Dreams, Reflections*

Contents

I Am Mostly Alone Here

Biograffiti

Moving out of the Attic

I Am Mostly Alone Here

Apricots

1

The woman in the window
is eating an apricot.
Her ruddy arm crosses the shadow
of her breast each time
she takes a bite.

2

In the kitchen of the yellow house
sunlight falls across
a dozen apricots in a blue bowl.
They light up from within,
glowing red and gold.

3

The man I love
is the color of ripe apricots.
I dream of biting
through his furred skin,
of sucking the thin clear juice.

4

Hello. Come in.
Won't you sit down?
I am mostly alone here.
Would you like
an apricot?

Montage

Here, the atmosphere
is stained with images
like a multiply exposed photograph.

I meet myself coming and going.

Past is a fiction we invent
to explain transparent faces
that float on the film like halos:

(I spoiled the focus.
My hand must have shaken.)

I am who I have been:

The girl who washes
the heavy red and white plate
at the white sink uses my hands.

Mother, Because We Do Not Speak of Such Things, I Have Written You a Poem

Mother, we are walking on the beach
just after sunset with my two children.
I pull the sagging sweater you knit
for me twelve years ago across my chest.

The sea is apple-jade now. Earlier today
the waves chewed at the sand
with white teeth: The children
flopped in them like flounders,
and every once in a while we took turns
reeling them in and rubbing them
with sandy towels until their lips reddened.
Now the sea is quiet and toothless,
an old lioness who runs a slow tongue
over the pebbles and breathes softly.

And we walk steadily. This is
my favorite time of day. I do not tell you
that. We have never spoken of such things.
You are telling me of the place, the people
I have left: I don't hear the details. What I hear
is the sound of your voice as steady
as the hiss of waves on this beach we
        have walked
summers ever since I can remember.

Mother, it is so peaceful here, with you,
now that I am going away.

Primipara

that night
we came apart
I
howling pain for both
your face
grinding against my sloped bones
you surfaced
to cold air the knife
the twist of cord against your belly
you
all screech and waul
outside of me
separate

now
not 9 years later
we are parted
by whatever volume of air
3000 miles holds
gulf white and blue
curve of brown earthskin
your voice
shivering
on a telephone cord
my name
clumsy on a white envelope

still
sometimes my hand
wanders over my belly
the palm
listening for your knock.

San Ildefonso

stones from the bellies
of dinosaurs
the women use
to polish the black pots

somewhere truly
beneath the ocean
a serpent's stirring
shakes the earth

throws up stones
into the streams

the black pots
twined with serpents
are rubbed with the old stones
once found in the water

the stones sacred
handed down
mother to daughter
never lost

The Invasion of the House by Tigers

The house has filled with tigers.
Two at the end of the hall roll
and lick each other's fur.
Over the baby's bed the breathing
of another stirs the zoo mobile.
I have heard one under the sink,
snuffling among the potatoes and dog food.

We hunker together with our heads down,
shoulders touching, and we put
the baby between us. But the frail
warmth of our skins frightens us.
We can't protect each other.

Separate in the dark we move
through the house, our fingers
stuck out, waiting to feel warm
saliva, teeth, a deep furred chest,
a hard huge yellow eye. We stumble
and whisper: Is that you? Is that you?
Did someone put the baby in his bed?
Where is the baby? Where
are you? Where is everyone?

Snapshot

On Children's Sunday
each child receives a geranium,
pink or red,
in a foil-covered pot.

Here I am
in white sailor hat with navy trim,
in white ankle socks and black patent-leather shoes,
holding a red geranium.

Jesus Loves Me.

But my father is dead.

For a Child Who Has Lost Her Cat

They go
you know:

no matter the dish of tinned tuna
the nest you build in your own quilts
the felt mouse
and the ball with pink and yellow stripes.

They disappear

into the paths of cars
into talons and beaks
into the arms of strangers
and the ravages of private disease

and from their leavings we learn
of leaving:

how everything that pads into our lives
soft-footed sleek
pads out again into the night
leaving traces.

(for Susan Abbey)

For All the Beautiful Boys

Oh but I love them
all the beautiful boys
love their thick hair
curling dark
around their narrow faces
love their throats
dusky in open collars
their torsos their fine
young cocks swelling their jeans
their buttocks (tight)
the muscles of their thighs
their heavy booted feet.

In the kindness
of dark and sleep I shed
the pale webs of my skin
my sleek grey hair
the musk of powder
and cologne. Whittled
hard and white as bone
I dress in silken skin
in heat in scent of oranges
and milk and then I love them
all the beautiful boys one
by one in the flame of my deep
woman hot insistent dreams.

Naming

Let me tell you this once
(I will not be able to say it again):
I have lost the meaning of words.
Heavy, they ripped away from the sounds,
fell into cracked ground. For weeks
I scratched but what I dug up was
bicycle spokes, black melon rinds,
a smashed doll face — it was not meaning.
I don't know what I am saying.

I exaggerate. Not everything is gone.
I still know perfectly what sugar means,
and pine needle. Laughter is more
of a problem. And yellow often slides,
a plate of butter in the sun.
The meaning of flower has gone entirely;
so has the meaning of love. Now it is safe
to say: I love you. Now it is true.

Wise

Solid, he is shadow
cast to stone against the candlelight.
My fingertips flare on his skin.
His weight burns and heals.

But dreams of such a man
eat through the flesh, chew
sinew and bone. Love of him
weights the eyelids with yellow coins.

He will not move his hand an inch
through the smoke:
He will outwait me.
My fingers wither under our eyes.

The man who doesn't love me
I love twice:
once for his beauty, again
for his sound sense.

Sung in a Dark House

At the doorway I squint into the sun and wave.
I return to arranging snapdragons
in a brass bowl and admiring my brown fingers
twisted among the red mouths.

It is better to resume loneliness quietly,
in a dark house. Each lover who leaves
leaves me surer to survive the next.

I know how to say goodbye with grace.
When the snapdragons wilt, I gather
dahlias, peonies, chrysanthemums.

I am only old. Love
will not have me for a friend.

Mechanic

Body as dwellingplace
of mind or soul, marrow, sheathed
nerves, ambiguous heart and spleen
makes no sense. We understand
what we can see:

an efficient tool
for perfecting the small gestures
of failed love.

The smile awry stuck to the teeth,
the snagged air, the wrists
burned by careless touch are, in time,
any lips, any breath, any hands.

Nothing fails utterly.
A man admired my hair once,
another my feet.
Such things have a meaning
however small,

however bitter.

Beast of My Heart

We live in this white and yellow space
just large enough
for a woman of bone and a black cat.

The woman: me.
The cat: ma Bête Noire,
the beast of my heart,

who eats the tip of my pen as I write,
who kills my apron hanging
beside the refrigerator in the night
when I am not awake to defend it.

Bête Noire is drowsing
on the latest revision of my latest short story
which will one day be rejected
in a personal letter by *The New Yorker*.

She is dreaming, I think,
of the Russian Blue in the next yard,
or of the doves whose feet scrabble on the roof,
or of me.

When I kill myself
I do it with a handful of tiny yellow pills.
Bête Noire sleeps against my feet
to keep us warm.

Desert Survival

One ocotillo
fanned against a grey rock fall

a clot of brittlebush

ironwood crouched
at the edge of a wash
crushed by light

that squeezes flesh through bone

and we strike out
suddenly
through the suboceanic pressure of heat

blood still salt

15,000 years collapses
on itself: Live here long enough
and you either swim or drown.

Figs

Don't pick before the buntings,
who know ripeness better than fingers
or tongue. Scarcely the size of figs,
they hop and peck through purple skin
to creamy flesh, taste sweetness,
reel away heavy, nearly drunk.
These are good figs.

Pick carefully.
Once the birds have opened
the figs' fat bellies the wasps crowd
golden and shiny as nectar drops
into each cavity. Turn each fig
lightly in your fingers.

Pick in time.
One day too late and you forfeit
to the green beetles who exist
only when figs exist. Their hard
iridescent bodies turn the fruit
into jewels of Fabergé. No one
will warn you of their arrival.
Like as not you'll guess it wrong.

Pick only what you can reach.
There is plenty. Don't covet
the fruit on the highest branches
which will be used all
but the skins. They will hang empty
and wrinkled as old men's testicles
right through till autumn.

Take all you need.
This is not your tree.

Earthly Delights

You write
that together we will take tea
in your garden, among the sweet william
and stocks, hollyhocks, pansies,
pots of thyme and savory, snapdragons:

jasmine in thin cups, a crock
of honey, crumbly shortbread.
On the wall behind you
sleeps a lizard, jeweled and gentle,
and two rosy finches bob under our feet.
Our dimity dresses flow milky
over pebbles of shadow.

When you explain to me that poet
of kingfishers and wrecked nights,
your voice stills, opens me,
bee-sweet. Your lips heat
the inside of my wrist.

Instead it is winter.
Your letters have stopped.
In the garden the bronze stems scraping
against the rimed grass bloom
with snow. Or
did they never grow?

The Night Visitor

Here is the dark one,
the one who lurks under the water
far out from the sandy edge
where the tadpoles squirm in the shadows,
far below the orange paddles of the wood ducks.
The one who makes you afraid to put your feet
all the way down.

He has come from the weedy pond
to the edge of your bed and turning you see
he is the color of amber,
he is lucid and smooth, warm to your fingers,
and his voice is not of tree frogs fretting the night
but is human, humorous,
and you unbend your knees.

Hospitality

When you come

I will put fresh flowers
in your room: in the ginger jar
daisies and black-eyed susans,
bits of fern, lavender,
if I can find it a yellow rose.

In the yellow kitchen
I will offer you coffee
and melon, a soft-boiled egg
with chives, honey on your toast.

If the day is cold, I will light
the fire, if warm, throw
the curtains and windows wide.

Do you carry the print
of these gestures in your head?

Do you think they're the same?

The Sleepers

How long a movement builds
before the first twitch.

I have watched for days
this bare heap where you put
eight squash seeds. Today
the earth splits, in the shadow
flickers the first green.

How do we begin to dream?

Cats dream us. You can watch
them do it in green
deep eyes. Snakes dream us
more with tongues.
It's easy for creatures. They also dream
each other, fish and mice,
sunlight, stretch of sinew, muscle —
right from birth.

Is it that they are mute?
Does speech murder sleep?

Surely a million times Iloveyou
flung in the air has rattled
and danced around us
like seeds, like rain clotting the dust.

But what grows,
what grows is not love —
no one, not the cleverest gardener,
can grow love — what grows is silence
that flowers, sets fruit, bears dreams.

One day your words stumbled
out of my mouth.
In my exhaustion, you dozed.

Nights I feel
your skin creep over me,
crush my chattering bones to quiet.
Now I can't say that I love you.
My tongue sleeps
between the shells of my jaws.

What we didn't know
before we slept is real:
There is no parting us now.

Biograffiti

Transcendence

She thought, I am always awaiting my moment of transcendence. It is always going to come at some other time. Why shouldn't it come now? Because I am sitting here drinking coffee and staring at this crumb of cracker caught in the pile of the gold rug. Because the cat is asleep, across from me, in the gold chair. In some other time, the gold chair would become perfect. Now it is just the gold chair, shabby, soiled, with a button missing and a gouge out of the wooden frame, with a cat asleep in it. In some other time the cat would be perfect, as he very nearly is but not quite, not quite, being just the lynx-point Siamese with the striped stockings who has always slept in this gold chair.

Education

She learned to be clever at Cleverness School. It was a rigorous course, and not everybody passed, but those who did had all the best things. She passed; in fact, she graduated with honors; and all were puzzled that she did not prosper.

The Juggler

She took up juggling. She practiced when no one was around, at first with one object, then with two, then three, until she could juggle as many as she liked.

One night she was juggling a dozen or more yellow balls for the entertainment of her friends. She tossed the balls higher and higher until, one by one, they disappeared over her head. Her friends stirred and murmured and exclaimed:

amazing
mazing
azing
zing
ing
ng
g!

She was delighted by the awe and admiration in their soft voices.

That night she went to bed late and fell directly to sleep. Some time later she was awakened in the dark by the thumping of the balls as they tumbled on the bed all around her.

The Toy

One afternoon, while she was taking a bath, she was as-tonished to see that a penis had grown between her legs. It bobbed beneath the surface of the scented water, reddish and rubbery, like a dog's toy.

Tentatively, she took hold of it. Her fingers in the oily water slipped against it agreeably, and it grew hard and thick. In the steamy heat she breathed rapidly, pressing her buttocks into the slick white enamel, and then groaned as the jet of milky fluid spurted though her fingers.

The penis withered quickly. Soon it fell off. When she pulled the plug, it disappeared into the whorl of the drain. She stood up and scrubbed her oiled skin with a red towel.

Dancers

The audience sat in the shadows outside the spotlighted circle of short green grass. Beyond was a bank of oleanders. She thought that the sparse flowers among the glossy dark foliage looked like stars at the beginning of night, but when she looked above her, the resemblance failed. She decided, being a safe distance from the ocean, that they were phosphorescent starfish trapped in seaweed.

Into this ring of poison leaped the dancers, shouting and gesticulating. They grew quiet. They began to move again, but slowly. Sometimes they wove intricacies, sometimes froze. Sometimes they made animal noises and other sounds, once raising the cry of thousands of voices twisted into the one voice of a woman gone insane. At that sound she saw suddenly a street in a large city, empty except for a wind scattering sheets of newspaper, a street carved out between the canyon walls of grey stone and flat glass, and she understood that the world would end.

Among all the dancers, who were not beautiful, she fell in love with one who was ugly. The dancer was thin, so thin that sharp shadows caught in the backs of her ankles and knees, in her collarbone, and her black leotard bagged over her buttocks. She was knock-kneed. Her short blonde hair was parted in the middle, yanked to either side and clamped with barrettes. In the spotlight her pale eyes glittered as they darted from one dancer to another, terrified of missing a motion, of failing to follow, of being the only one to turn left and leap when the others sagged right and collapsed.

She loved this dancer more than the others, but she loved all of them some, as much as she could, being in the shadows.

Felo-de-se

She took to drawing sharp objects across the insides of her wrists: fragments of amber glass; tiny pearl-handled silver knives; single-edged razor blades. Again and again, in a gesture smooth and submerged as a dancer's, she practiced the sweep across one track of blue veins, the other.

When she inclined her head to the question of a friend. In the supermarket checkout line, buying grapes. As she tied the baby's shoes. At orgasm. At her sister's wedding. At the punch-line of a joke.

The wrists opened, bloodless, as fresh and pink as small mouths, closed again. Finally, discouraged by the lack of effect, she ceased.

Vaccination

She had, it turned out, a weakness for beautiful Jewish boys
from Harvard. Fortunately, a vaccine had been developed
which provided immunity from this disorder. The vaccine was
live, however, and made her at first ill to the point of death. It
was nonetheless effective. The wound healed and left a scar
no more disfiguring than the small silvery coin of her smallpox
vaccination or the point marking the old entry of a friends's
toy arrow.

Names

When, rarely, she was alone in the house, she moved from object to object, giving each one a name. Couch. Table. Hairbrush. Plant: schefflera. Lamp. Plant: croton. Chest. Chair.

She was never entirely alone, because the creatures were there. But they had no words, so in this way they were no help but rather a responsibility. They had to be named as well. Cat: Gwydion. Snake: Hroðgar. Mouse: Bittersweet. Dog: Amaroq. The baby mice, who were food for the snakes, had no names, but they had to be labeled mice lest they be something else.

However rapidly she worked was never fast enough. As soon as she had named bed and moved to typewriter, the bed was dissolving. She could keep the objects going in one room at a time, not more.

When the others were there, it was much easier. They went around in the parts of the house where she wasn't and named things she was too busy to get to. But whenever she was alone she wound up weak and half crying with exhaustion from all the responsibility.

The Purple House

At one time, she considered painting her house purple, but nothing ever came of it.

Parts

Walking on the sidewalk in the middle of the day, she felt her body growing heatstruck and heavy. The light bunched at the nape of her neck, dragged at her buttocks, pummeled the backs of her knees. She could feel canvas bags, stuffed with chunks of sunrock and strung to her shoulders, her wrists, thumping against her thighs.

She began to let go. At first she released just the forefinger of her left hand, but even that almost imperceptible weight made a difference, so she let the whole hand go. Then the other. Piece after piece, as her stride lightened and then ceased.

When she became aware of her lightness, she looked down and was startled to see that her whole body had disappeared. She turned slowly. Along the sidewalk behind her were the various parts.

She thought: *It really isn't fair. They mean well in spite of the trouble they've caused.* Still slowly, she returned along the sidewalk, picking up the pieces and attaching them. The little finger of the left hand had been slightly mashed by a careless boot. She straightened it carefully and the damage hardly showed.

The End of Love

Once, she fell in love. It was, she thought, the most remarkable, the most delightful state she had ever experienced: a state rather like possession but purified of satanic overtones (because her beloved was a good, pleasant man who had no idea that she had a soul, much less any designs upon it).

She discovered that, indeed, her heart was the seat of her passions. She could feel it swell and heave against her ribs, choking her at times with its hot mass. From it stretched fibers tight as tuned piano wires which resonated at his any glance, the stroke of his voice. She was translated into a sonata, wordless and gorgeous.

All this was very well.

On a Wednesday afternoon in late spring, she and her beloved were striding across a field on their way to the museum, where they would improve their minds. She removed, momentarily, her eyes from his tawny profile in order to avoid stumbling and glimpsed to her right a clump of red and ragged flame. *Look!* she cried. *Look at the poppies!* He peered about him, nearsighted. *Poppies,* he said. *Ah. Hmm. So those are poppies. I never notice such things.*

Pseudocyesis

Each time, her breasts swelled, grew tender, the nipples hard and brown. Her period stopped. A dark line formed between navel and pubis. Then her belly rounded, the stretched skin marked by silvery snail tracks. Under her palms curved to the roundness she could feel the lurch and wriggle of a fingerling trout.

At this point, each time, her belly and breasts collapsed like balloons kept around too long after a little girl's birthday party.

The Tail

Later, she realized that it was the happiest decision of her life, the decision to grow a tail. It meant to her that she no longer had to mind certain significant differences. She was, in fact, different from everyone else. People didn't have tails, and she did.

It took some getting used to. At first, when her son came close to examine it, she fretted: *Be careful of my tail.* But soon he was combing it and tying it in knots. They decided that the knots weren't very pretty, but when he tied a bow in the end, it looked quite fine.

So sometimes she wore it in a bow and sometimes just plain. It was about four feet long, covered with soft brown fur. Most of the time, when she was sitting, as she usually was, she wrapped it tightly, warmly, around her ankles so that no one would step on it.

It gave her immeasurable comfort. She took to smiling unexpectedly.

The Ice Palace

In the winter a man built her a palace of ice, in which she lived alone.

During the day, because there were no windows, the light filtering through the rough blocks was glassy and grey. She could not always tell whether the sun was shining outside. She never went out to see, though she was not in any way held prisoner. The man sent her daily roses that gaped in the submarine twilight, and she dreamed of drowning. She breathed little, and when she did, her breathing made no sound. She moved little, also, and slowly against the weight of the light.

At night the walls turned black. Reflecting the points of the hundeds of candle flames, they seemed mirror-shallow; but when she stared into them, they grew infinitely thick. The roses, in the candlelight, were bloody, and they made little breathy sounds when she went near them, exuding the velvety scent that she associated with the inside of her thighs.

Unable, of course, to have a fire, she was wrapped day and night in a heavy chill that took away desire to sleep or eat. But the man had given her several rugs of sable, one of which she kept always around her, so that she was never uncomfortable. There was, deep inside her, a red point, a coal, which the ice preserved perfectly.

That spring, there was an unusually early thaw. Then she had to go elsewhere to live.

Moving out of the Attic

In the Dry Season

Here
is need
for the forgiveness of rain.

Green greyed
by dust and the white sear of sun
flesh shrivels
ground cracked at the root.

Here
the dry vigil

of the snake
milk-eyed
within the shadow of stone

of the seed split

the wait
for the rustle in brittlebush
in mesquite
for the fragrance of stirred dust

signifying rain.

Bless me:
I have thorns.

Bless me.
I have bitter water
at my heart.

The Old Teiresias

1

A young man, walking alone,
I came upon two snakes green, slender,
their tongues and eyes like onyx,
in the slow coils of copulation; stood entranced
a moment before I ripped the two apart
and felt at the same time
my cock wizen into my widening thighs,
my breasts grow heavy, tender.

And it was horrible—I can't tell you,
can't tell you how horrible the disfigurement,
the wound slashed between my legs, sensitive,
moist, smelling of low tide and crustaceans, bleeding
sometimes, the soft clots blooming like anemones.

There was a coil of darkness in my brain
that unwound and spread through my belly, down my thighs,
a slow black spreading silence opening me,
as unlike the quick bright flash of maleness
as summer lightning is to the ocean at midnight.

All the same, I was glad to go back.

2

That silly marital argument might
have been shaped in the brain of Aristophanes:

He: *You women have all the luck. You shiver
       in the spasms of love hours after we are spent.*

She: *Ah, but your male moment, though brief,
       shoots fire like all the stars of heaven.*

He: *No, my dear, women's is the greater pleasure.*
She: *You're wrong.*
                  He: You're *wrong.*
She: *Not on your life.*
                 He: *We'll give it to Teiresias.*
I (tremulous. Remember who I'd been.
   It wasn't even a calculated risk): *Women.*

I was lucky to get away with blindness.

3

If he had left well enough alone,
blindness would have been the worst of it. But no:
I had to have recompense, this other vision that stains
my darkness with possibility: hard death, harder
afterlife, pulled back to blood even from eternity
to have my knowing plucked from my brain
like eyeballs from their sockets

and still no power to lie.

To the Crossers of Night

1

The root
in the belly
blackened and tenacious

the green shoot
splitting ribs

the bulbed eyesockets

at the back of the tongue
the earth
rich with decay

and the petaled pale unfurling
of fingers:

in this difficult landscape
what grows
bears pain.

2

Before the rain

                          peace.

After the rain

                          peace.

Under the lilacs that grew
    by your mother's doorway

                          peace.

In the black heart of the red poppy

                          peace.

Beneath the startled wing
    of the swift

                          peace.

In all the rooms of the yellow
    house

                          peace.

3

Horses that come
to drink in your pool
fall in and drown.

Snakes come
to the back door of the yellow house
to be fed.

Nothing but cactus grows
at the feet
of the painted priests.

Through a small square cut
in cardboard you see,
once, the universe.

4

Of the child in the stone
in the shaft of light
peeping between the lilies

say little.

Of the man with the blue iris
who stands on the cliff
above the grey ocean

say less.

Conversations at All Hours

1

o dead father
do you know
I am a decade older
than you were when you died

ten years beyond you

the grey springs from my scalp
vivid as wires
that pick up intimations in all weathers

my nerves sing high-pitched, tuneless

and sometime now
they sing of death

2

they tell me
when you died
I cried

and would not leave the place above which
you had soared:
Heaven a hole in the blue canvas
over palms and pounded coral

until they told me you
would come too no matter
where I moved

since then I have dragged you
weightless frail balloon at the end
of a tether

where you might never have wished to go
on your own

and anchored you
in each new room
above the mirror on my dresser

3

they tell me
I wear your face

I do not know

in the snapshot
your head is thrown back
collar open at the throat
you are smiling

at your elbow my face
within the heavy fringes of hair
is tight as a peony bud
pink and petaled over

though not with pain

4

I wear the ring
you gave my mother
on the third finger of my right hand

clot of gold

its weight drags at my bones
holds me a little closer
to the earth's core

5

of the times you have loved me
of the times you have failed to love me
I have lost count

I have had the love
of one good man:
I did not think it enough

my hunger I keep wrapped in lilacs
and in the memory of lilacs

at times
I have thought I would die of it

6

gravid I have moved
with gestures as slow as though through water
as though I were the fetus
turning in the darkened fluid

I have borne you children: two:

they are strange to me
their faces open and jeweled
as day lilies

they believe that no one will ever leave them
without stopping first
to say goodbye

7

pulled down now
by illness
this long dream

I scuttle and tack
black crab among fronds
on the floor of a murky ocean

I can not plan
on rising

To Virginia (and Points West)

1

"how the dead sing behind rhododendron bushes"
V.W., *Mrs. Dalloway*

Everything, in time,
takes very long.

The press of white lawn
against white stocking, the curve
of breast, shoulder, the stiff feathers
of the birdie shot from the racquet
—thwack!—dove-white against the sky.

He lies on his back in the grass
under the elm, blazer open,
one arm thrown across his eyes.

None of this,
I promise you, is true.

Under the bridge the fish hang
in the water, slips of silver, heads
turned upstream. He leans out,
imagining himself a fish, the brown water
against his flanks. He feeds on minnows.

She leans further, imagining herself
Ophelia, turning slowly in the pinnace
of her white garments downstream,
scattering dead-men's-fingers, dirty songs.

There is a miracle.
It is no longer fashionable
to name it.
It was called love.

She waits in the shadows
for the first touch. Her skin is whiter
than the dress at her feet.
When his fingers stroke her breasts
they tremble and swing like mute bells.

Not until death do we
enter an eternity of song.

2

"we know not why we go upstairs, or why we come down again"
V.W., *Orlando*

In the morning
I rescue a toad from a pool of brown water
and put him under the squash leaves.

Later I find him
halfway engorged by a striped
garter snake.

Excusing myself,
I twist three furry zucchinis
from their stalks, carry them
into the kitchen for supper.

Now I hear
someone knocking at the front door.
If I answered, I could ask:
Why have you come here?

A light mist pearls
above the alfalfa field. The drops
on the nacreous flesh of the cut zucchinis
wet my fingers, the knife.

Light fails. The dragons
have fallen asleep
at the bottom of the garden.

3

"But still — I eat up the black and doubtful pieces of meat in memory — "
                                        V. W. , *Letters*

Fixed,

a retinal burn in time:

On dry pine needles, the sky
pewter through the thinning trees,
she tries to spread her legs
shackled by terror.

The scene enacts, reenacts
itself (the butting cock, the knees
arthritic with fear). No matter:

that she dreams of orgasm
in the arms of a giant
the color of clay, whimpers once,
wakes with eyes empty as the sky;

that he
has gone to West Virginia again
to think.

4

"others are hundreds of years old though they call themselves thirty-six"
                                                V.W., *Orlando*

Next week
at the dark of the moon
I turn thirty-six.

The bats will swoop,
chittering, from the barns, the trees,
and cover my eyes
tight with their leathery wings.

From the tall grass
the fox will come up,
parting the blades with his sharp nose,
and bite my throat.

I will turn and turn
forever blind and dumb in the tug
of earth under the absence of moon.

5

"I am old; I am ugly. I am repeating things."
V.W., A Writer's Diary

In the dusk bats drop
and flitter over a theatre of grass.

There are fireflies
among the burning poppies.

No hand touches my chill skin
except in dreams.

I might
have lived another life.

After Spring

1

in the spines
of the saguaros the wind
whines
the spines voiceless
are sung

word makes
the saguaros these
wreathed brides
wax flowers on their heads, their arms

virgin voices
singing epithalamia

2

dust dances
in devils

flesh on the skeleton
of the wind

3

that scours mountains
to bone
and sings them

4

I have become
part of the landscape that didn't produce me
bones scoured

an Aeolian harp
for the breath of the wind going through
my rib cage
out of my mouth

the words
that the wind
which is not wind but spirit
insists upon

5

the word speaks the word
gives life

spiny song of spirit

saguaro dust mountain
rib cage
mouth

6

word silent
my integuments dissolve

bones grinding to dust
at the edge
of a wash in the season before the rains

under a quiet saguaro
that wears burst fruit blood-blackened
by the moon

Moving out of the Attic

1. Metamorph

In the dark
from a dream of rain black
and new green

she wakes to the touch
of a stranger
in the arms of a stranger

who holds her too hard
bone of his shoulder bruising
the bone of her cheek.

Snared, stilled
in the cave of black
quilt, of heat, she lies

the bruise spreading deep:
becomes stranger to herself
a woman who breathes in dream

(the old self loosed, rising
against the dark, chilled
and bitter as rain)

knows that she has been loved
by a man who loved her only in sleep
dreaming her someone else.

2. In Sleep

All night the moan of trains stitches
the ragged edges of my dreams.

Two strangers sleep in this bed with me: you
and the woman clasped against your breathing
who wears my warm flesh heavily.

Time, split by train whistle, falls open,
away, leaves us pearled in light: the glass coffin.

I dream that you put in my lap
a black and white kitten. I dream then
that you tell me you love me.

In the morning when you wake me from this dream,
give me grapefruit juice and the news,
I will hear without hearing a train howl.

Leaving you, I will bear in my flesh the needle
of dream, a single splinter struck from glass.

3. Memory: Love:

In the yellow afternoon I watch
your eyes (green
as the glass that washes up
on New Hampshire beaches):

behind them
a dead brother, a lover who married someone else,
the Brattle Theatre,
a clump of reeds against a screen of sumac
(the Berkshires, October).

These
made into words sting
like poison, drug like poison.

Memory: love:
bitter itch from the whip of your words,
your laughter, your face turning away,

away.

I trace
the hollow between your neck and shoulder
honing words
to slip like razors under your skin.

I am as speechless as the dead.

I would kill you
if I could

I will kill you
as soon as I can.

4. Someone Else's Nightmare

You hand me my costume:
the talons, the teeth.
I have forgotten what to do with them.

You slip them into place,
push me into position center stage.

Spotlights stain the space
behind my eyelids violet, rose.
These colors are wrong.

Opening my eyes, I see
that you have taken up
the white sword.

I will not be
in someone else's nightmare.

I strip to a bare body,
warm skin over warm flesh, and walk
through an opening window into the desert.

I have my own nightmares: I am,
for instance, afraid of thirst, of the dark.

5. April. The Sudden Heat.

Into the trill and stutter
of mockingbirds awake at this wrong hour
all night throats open, eyes wide

I rouse to see a woman's face
I will never wear
moon-pale rising

against the viscid surface
of a night otherwise dark
fretted by song.

I think of beginnings:
new heat, one finger on a wrist,
the stark wet instant of conception.

It is like thinking of you dead
your face stony, prophetic,
given over to long dreams

and some light,
resinous, fixing the shadows
along your mouth in amber

or of myself dead
long weeds wound around throat and fingers
with pearls for eyes

and beyond, the grey wakeful birds
thrilling crazily:
epithalamia at two o'clock and three o'clock.

6. A Waking

In the pleasant dream
I rock in the pool from the yellow lamp
in my lap the book of poems
and the cat with striped mask and striped stockings

warm
and the dark beyond still
but for the whippoorwill at nine o'clock
the whir of bats.

Here the cat's purr
stirs the silence into small waves.

Your face emerging indistinct
among the yellow daisies in the brown jar

wakes, moves me
under the weight of memory and the lost tomorrow
to the open door
down the long mown meadow

to find myself reduced
to this crabbed scratching under soil
for the word difficult enough
to be your name.

7. A Revision

In this book
I am in love with you.

I cannot help myself:
I am the central female character.

Who wrote this book?

You tell me, "Men never know
they're in love till it's over."

Whoever wrote my book
wrote yours.

But
there is another text:

In it
I live in a yellow house on the coast of Maine.
The garden is filled with day lilies.

Each morning I cut the sprays
and put them in the blue hobnail pitcher
on the kitchen windowsill.

The rest of each day
is suffused with orange and yellow light.

8. Outside

In a cold country breath clouds
into a shadow face
kissing at the mouth

the cold kiss
drawing blood through pale lips

red blooming on snow
the lost heart
the rose.

The task
is to be ready when winter
is ready

is to be lifted
impaled
on the brutal horn:

outside all books
outside all dreams and memory
of dreams

what love lasts
forever?

The Departure of the Women

The men trample the earth.
Beneath their huge feet the dust
puffs in swollen balls
that burst on their chests.
Their hands swing slow arcs
against the brown air. Under old
sun their furred torsos are
red boles in the hot wind.
Their penises, strangled
serpents, slap their thighs right
left. Their buttocks clench.

Where are the women?
Have they gone to the well?
Have they gone to the war?
They are hidden
like water. They have become
the blue fluid that oozes
from under rocks and lies
beside them dark and quiet.
They have become the other
rocks. Tired, tired, strong,
they are seeping
back into the earth alone.